MAKING
GREAT

Tags, Tags,
Boxes
&
Cards

MAKING GREAT
Bags, Tags, Boxes & Cards

Karen Delquadro

Sterling Publishing Co., Inc., New York

A Sterling/Chapelle Book

Chapelle, Ltd.:
Jo Packham
Sara Toliver
Cindy Stoeckl

Editor: Kelly Ashkettle
Book Designer: Rose Sheifer
Art Director: Karla Haberstich
Copy Editors: Marilyn Goff/Anne Bruns
Graphic Illustrator: Kim Taylor
Staff: Areta Bingham, Donna Chambers,
Emily Frandsen, Lana Hall,
Susan Jorgensen, Jennifer Luman,
Melissa Maynard, Barbara Milburn,
Lecia Monsen, Suzy Skadburg,
Linda Venditti, Desirée Wybrow

Designer: Paige Hill. Pages 16–17, 20–21,
24–25, 30–35, 40–41, 54–55, 60–61, 70–81,
87, 94–95, 100, 109–110, 114, 122–126.

Library of Congress Cataloging-in-Publication Data
Delquadro, Karen
Making great bags, tags, boxes & cards / Karen Delquadro.
p. cm.
Includes index.
ISBN 1-4027-0921-8
1. Gift wrapping 2. Greeting cards. 3. Box making. I. Title.
TT870.D3656 2004
745.54—dc22
2004003339

10 9 8 7 6 5 4 3 2 1

Published in paperback in 2005 by Sterling Publishing Co., Inc.
387 Park Avenue South, New York, NY 10016
© 2004 by Karen Delquadro
Distributed in Canada by Sterling Publishing
℅ Canadian Manda Group, 165 Dufferin Street,
Toronto, Ontario, Canada M6K 3H6
Distributed in Great Britain by Chrysalis Books Group PLC, The
Chrysalis Building, Bramley Road, London W10 6SP, England
Distributed in Australia by Capricorn Link (Australia) Pty. Ltd.
P. O. Box 704, Windsor, NSW 2756, Australia

Printed in China
All Rights Reserved

Sterling ISBN 1-4027-0921-8 Hardcover
         ISBN 1-4027-2779-8 Paperback

For information about custom editions, special sales, premium
and corporate purchases, please contact Sterling Special Sales
Department at 800-805-5489 or specialsales@sterlingpub.com.

Every effort has been made to ensure that all information in this book is accurate. However, due to differing conditions, tools, and individual skills, the publisher cannot be responsible for any injuries, losses, and/or damages which may result from the use of the information in this book.

This volume is meant to stimulate ideas. If readers are unfamiliar or not proficient in a skill necessary to attempt a project, we urge that they refer to an instructional book that specifically addresses the technique.

For questions or comments, contact:
Chapelle, Ltd., Inc.
P.O. Box 9252
Ogden, UT 84409
(801) 621-2777
(801) 621-2788 Fax
e-mail: chapelle@chapelleltd.com
web site: www.chapelleltd.com

Space would not permit the inclusion of every decorative item photographed for this book, nor could all of the designers be identified. Many of these items may be referred to on the Ruby & Begonia web site: www.rubyandbegonia.com or by calling (801)334-7829.

Dedication

To my Olivia, who inspires me every moment of my life. To my mother, who taught me the importance of presentation. To Debra, who was my gift-packaging mentor. To Scarlett, Kim, and Tamara, who have sung my praises from the beginning. And most of all, to Oprah, who through the magic of television, inspired me to find the courage to take a chance on believing in myself.

Karen

Table of Contents

Karen Delquadro is an accomplished scrapbooker who enjoys creating personalized items to fit featured themes or events. When it comes to giving gifts, she often has difficulty finding the perfect packaging in a store, so she came up with a solution: creating her own! In this book, Karen uses many of the same materials she uses for her scrapbooking (such as decorative papers, tags, stickers, embellishments, and die cuts) to coordinate the packaging of her gifts.

Designer Paige Hill has also contributed to this book with ideas for packaging that is part of the gift itself— metal cooling racks wired together to create a basket for various kitchen items, a colorful plastic suitcase packed with necessary items for a new baby, and a vintage teacup lovingly filled with favorite teas, to name a few.

Designing your own packaging can also be lighter on the wallet. For example, a large ream of colored card stock is less than $10.00 and you can create hundreds of cards from it. With a typical store-bought card costing about $4.00, you can see how the savings add up!

The materials list for each project in this book contains everything necessary to complete all of the coordinated pieces of that project. If you choose to make only one or two pieces in a project, a quick read through the instructions should enable you to easily pick from the materials list what you will need. Also, specific dimensions were seldom given, allowing you to create the proper size packaging for your individual gifts.

It is our hope that by exploring the techniques in this book, you will learn to better express and share your creativity with the special people in your life.

Chapter One

All Occasions

Thank You

Materials

- ⅛" hole punch
- ½" hole punch
- ¾" square punch
- 4 pink mini brads
- 8" green string
- Card stocks: light pink, dark pink, and lime green
- Daisy punch
- Floral-patterned decorative paper
- Glue dots
- Glue stick
- Mints or candy
- Pink floral mini brads
- Pink ink pad
- Ruler
- Scissors
- Small, sheer, white drawstring bag
- "Thank you" stamp
- Vellum
- White scrap paper

Bag

1. Fill bag with mints or candy of choice.
   Option: If you choose to make bag, see "Believe" on page 36 for instructions.

Tag

1. Cut out tag from dark pink card stock.
2. Punch one green circle with ½" punch and glue to the top of the tag.
3. Using ⅛" hole punch, punch hole through green circle. Tie green string through hole.
4. Punch three light pink and three green squares.
5. Attach to bottom of tag with glue dots, alternating the colors.
6. Punch one vellum daisy and one white paper daisy. Place paper daisy on top of vellum daisy and attach with pink floral brad to bottom-left corner of tag.

Card

1. Cut card from green card stock. Fold in half.
2. Using glue stick, add floral paper to top of card, leaving green strip of card showing on bottom.
3. Using daisy punch, punch three daisy shapes from vellum. Space evenly on green strip on card bottom.
4. Using daisy punch, punch three daisy shapes out of white paper. Place a paper daisy on top of each vellum daisy and secure each with a pink mini brad.
5. Using pink ink, stamp "Thank you" on inside of card.
6. Let dry before closing.

Many Thanks

Materials

- 2 dominoes
- 4¾" waxed envelope
- Bamboo tree stamp
- Black fuzzy thread
- Black permanent ink pad
- Brown card stock
- Coordinating textured paper
- Decorative paper with a Chinese writing pattern and a blank border
- Glue dots
- Glue stick
- Manila tag
- Mini alphabet stamps
- Ruler
- Scissors
- Small gift box

Box

1. Cover lid of box with the decorative paper, attaching with glue stick.
2. Cover bottom half of box with matching plain decorative paper, attaching with glue stick. Let dry, and insert the present.
3. Place lid on box and wrap fuzzy thread around center of box several times, tying ends together at top.
4. Cover knot with domino by attaching with glue dot.

Tag

1. Cut decorative paper to fit front of manila tag and attach to manila tag with glue stick.
2. Wrap fuzzy thread around bottom of tag and attach domino on left front of string with glue dots.
3. Loop fuzzy thread through hole in tag and tie.

Card

1. Cut a 1½" x 3¾" rectangle from card stock. Cut a 1½" x 3¾" rectangle from decorative paper with a blank border running down one long edge. Using glue dots, attach rectangle of decorative paper to rectangle of card stock, with decorative side up.
2. Using mini alphabet stamps, stamp "Many Thanks" in the blank border.
3. Stamp the bamboo tree pattern down the side of waxed envelope.

You're My Cup of Tea

Materials

- 1 yard mesh ribbon
- 2 vintage velvet flowers
- Floral sticker or image
- Glue gun
- Pop dot
- Sewing machine
- Silk ribbon
- Tea bags
- Teacup and saucer
- Vellum
- Victorian calling card

Container

1. Hot-glue mesh ribbon in center of saucer underside.
2. Make vellum envelopes to hold tea bags by sewing two pieces of vellum together at the sides and bottom, inserting tea bags, and folding over top. Tie with silk ribbon and add a small velvet flower.
3. Place tea bags in teacup and place on saucer. Hot-glue velvet flower to side of teacup. (This can be easily removed later so that the cup can be used.)

Tag

1. Attach floral sticker or image to front of calling card, using a pop dot.
2. Tie card onto tea bags with silk ribbon.
3. Bring the ends of mesh ribbon up over the teacup, and tie a bow.

Materials

- ⅛" hole punch
- ½" hole punch
- 1" square punch
- Black fine-tipped marker
- Black ink pad
- Card stock: 3 shades of brown
- Clear craft glue
- Decorative "brick" paper
- Foam squares
- Glue dots
- Glue stick
- Natural-colored raffia
- Paper bag
- Pewter "Friends" charm
- Ruler
- Rust-colored mini brads
- Scissors
- Small twigs
- Twine
- Various-sized alphabet stamps

Bag

1. Cut a 2½" x 6½" strip of light brown card stock and add brads to each corner.
2. Stamp "Welcome" on strip in large letters and attach strip to bag with foam squares.
3. Fill bag with "welcome to the neighborhood" items.

Card

1. Cut card out of medium brown card stock. Fold in half.
2. Using craft glue, attach two strips of twine horizontally in center of card front. Let dry.
3. Punch three 1" squares out of dark brown card stock. Evenly space and attach with foam squares on the top of the twine.
4. Make bundle of straw from raffia and attach to first square with craft glue.
5. Make bundle of the twigs and attach to second square with craft glue.
6. Cut a square of brick paper slightly smaller than the third square and attach with glue stick. Cut out three more bricks from brick paper and attach to brick paper with foam squares for a 3-D effect.
7. Cut a strip of dark brown card stock and attach with glue stick to center of card beneath the three squares.
8. Cut a strip of light brown card stock. Stamp "straw, twigs, brick" with the small alphabet stamps. Attach light brown strip with glue stick to the center of dark brown strip.

1. Cut tag from medium brown card stock.
2. Fold bottom of tag over about 1" and secure with mini brads to create a pocket.
3. Using marker, add border with dash-dot-dot technique.
4. Using glue stick, cover the pocket with brick paper. Cut out the individual bricks and attach with foam squares for a 3-D effect.
5. Place the corner of "friends" charm in the pocket. Secure with glue dots.
6. Punch one brown circle with ½" punch and glue to top of tag. Punch hole through brown circle with ⅛" hole punch. Tie twine through hole.

Kitchen Basket

Basket

1. Using the wire, attach the three cooling racks together at the corners, forming a bottom and two sides.
2. Place the kitchen items in the desired fashion in the wire "basket." Secure with raffia.

Card

1. Cut two pieces of equal-sized patterned paper and place wrong sides together.
2. Using a pin, make six small holes on left side of paper.
3. Thread needle with linen thread and whipstitch around the card through holes.
4. Cut a coordinating piece of patterned paper to fit the card front and attach with glue stick.
5. Attach the printed saying, using a pop dot.
6. Type greeting onto vellum and tear into small strip.
7. Attach to front of card with mini brads.
8. Hot-glue flower accent in place above greeting.

Materials

- 2 mini brads
- 3 square wire cooling racks
- Embroidery needle
- Excelsior
- Glue gun
- Glue stick
- Kitchen items
- Linen thread
- Patterned paper
- Pin
- Pop dot
- Printed greeting
- Raffia
- Small flower accent
- Vellum
- Wire

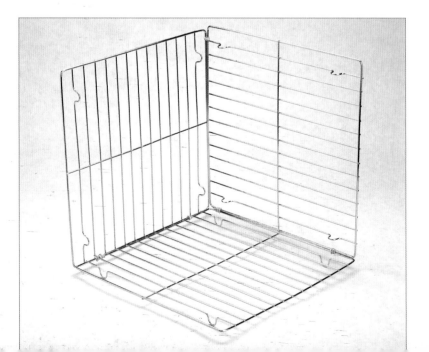

I AWOKE THIS MORNING
WITH DEVOUT THANKSGIVING
FOR MY FRIENDS.
RALPH WALDO EMERSON

THANK YOU

Materials

- ⅛" hole punch
- ½" hole punch
- 1" circle punch
- 1" square punch
- Alphabet stamps
- Black alphabet stickers
- Black felt-tipped marker
- Black ink pad
- Card stocks: orange, black, red, and yellow
- Kite string
- Mini glue dots
- Orange metal-rimmed tag
- Orange paper bag
- Paper butterfly
- Paper dragonfly
- Ruler
- Scissors

Bag

1. Glue string horizontally across bottom of bag, about one-fourth of the way up.
2. Cut three orange squares and attach to bag with mini glue dots, spacing evenly.
3. Glue a dragonfly to the first square and a butterfly to the third square.
4. Make a ladybug for the center square by punching a 1" red circle and cutting it in half to form wings. Punch three ⅛" holes randomly in each wing.
5. Punch a 1" black circle to form the body. Glue wings to top of body, making the wings touch at the top and spread out into an inverted "V" shape.
6. Punch a ½" black circle for the head, and glue to the underside of the 1" black circle, allowing 90 percent to stick out.
7. Punch two white ⅛" circles for eyes. Add black dots for pupils, using a felt-tipped marker. Attach eyes to head with mini glue dots.
8. Glue ladybug to center square.

Tag

1. Stamp recipient's name on metal-rimmed tag.
2. Make a ladybug as described in bag instructions above and glue to corner of tag. Tie string through hole.

Card

1. Cut card from orange card stock. Fold in half.
2. Cut strip of yellow card stock and glue to card front.
3. Apply stickers to card front to spell "Buggy for You."
4. Make a ladybug as described in bag instructions above, and glue to right side of card.

Bathed in Glory

Materials

- Circular soap
- Excelsior
- Glue gun
- Gold cup hook
- Planter
- Ribbon
- Stationery
- Silk flowers
- Small frame

Box

1. Using a glue gun, apply the flowers all along the outside edge of the planter, alternating colors and styles. Option: Try using planters in a variety of shapes, sizes, and colors.
2. Place the desired amount of excelsior in the bottom of the planter and place the soaps inside.
3. Wrap ribbon over soap and glue to the base of the planter, leaving about 1" of ribbon.

Tag

1. Type a greeting on stationery. Cut to size of frame and glue inside with glue gun.
2. Attach gold cup hook to back of frame, using glue gun.
3. Attach frame to planter with glue gun.

CONGRATULATIONS
MARY ANNE
SINCERELY
ELIZABETH OLSEN

Bride and Groom

Materials

- "&" stamp
- ¼" hole punch
- 2 metal nameplates
- 3 white thumbtacks
- Brown card stock
- Brown ink pad
- Brown lunch-pail-style cardboard box
- Cardboard mailing tag
- Cream-colored tulle
- Glue dots
- Glue gun
- Large brown-tinted flower with leaves
- Paintbrush
- Ruler
- Sandpaper or emery board
- Scissors
- Small brown wooden heart
- Small heart stamp
- Various-sized alphabet stamps
- White paint
- Wire cutters

Box

1. Hot-glue flower and leaves to side of box.

Tag

1. Attach nameplate at top of tag, on a horizontal slant.
2. Stamp "bride" in window with brown ink.
3. Lightly paint front of wooden heart with white paint so some brown shows through. Let dry.
4. Paint white over a small area of bottom of tag. Let dry.
5. Snip off heads of three thumbtacks with wire cutters.
6. Attach heads to right edge of card with glue dots.
7. Sand edges of paint from wooden heart for rustic look.
8. Stamp "&" on heart with brown ink.
9. Stamp "groom" on white paint with brown ink, using various sizes of stamps.
10. Attach tulle through hole in tag.

Card

1. Cut card from brown card stock. Fold in half.
2. Paint a small rectangular section of the card front white, using uneven strokes.
3. Attach nameplate vertically to lower-left corner of card, using glue dots.
4. Stamp small hearts in window, using brown ink.
5. Stamp "LOVE" on painted square with brown ink.
6. Punch two ¼" holes through top of card, ¾" apart.
7. Attach tulle through holes and tie bow.

Materials

- ¼" hole punch
- 8" kite string
- Alphabet stamps
- Baby blue card stock
- Black ink pad
- Blue crafting chalk
- Blue decorative paper
- Blue mini plastic pacifier
- Blue striped gift bag
- Footprint stamps
- Glue stick
- Handprint stamps
- Large blue brads
- Nursery rhyme stickers
- Scissors
- Small and large square punches
- Small lamb stickers
- Vellum

Bag

1. Tear vellum in half and on a slight angle. Measure width of bag and trim vellum accordingly. Attach vellum to bag with large blue brads, forming a pocket.

Tag

1. Cut tag from baby blue card stock. Punch top of tag with ¼" hole punch.
2. Glue decorative paper to bottom half of tag.
3. Stamp handprints on lower-right side with black ink.
4. Punch three small blue squares and attach to the left side of tag.
5. Place lamb stickers on each square.
6. Stamp "boy" on the angled portion of tag.
7. Thread kite string through hole of tag. Tie ends around plastic pacifier and attach to bag.
8. Tear word or symbol from decorative paper. Chalk edges of torn paper with blue craft chalk and attach with glue stick to string above pacifier.

Card

1. Cut card from baby blue card stock.
2. Tear decorative paper slightly smaller than the size of the card and glue to card front.
3. Punch large blue square. Glue to lower-left corner of card. Add sticker to top of square.
4. Cut a piece of blue card stock about the width of the card and stamp "congratulations" on it. Glue it on card front at an angle. Stamp baby footprints on lower-right corner of card with black ink.

Bag

1. Cut two 12" x 18" pieces and two 4½" x 21" straps of decorator fabric, four 3½" x 18" pieces of contrasting fabric, and four 18" lengths of trim.
2. Sew a contrasting strip to the top and bottom edges of each 12" x 18" panel. Press all seam allowances.
3. Sew trim along all seam allowances.
4. Sew strap pieces together, right sides in, then turn right sides out and press.
5. Fold the top contrasting piece down with wrong sides together. Pin the handle where you would like it to go and sew the folded fabric down. Repeat with the other panel and handle.
6. Sew the two panels together, being careful to match seams. Sew a loop of trim into the right-hand seam.
7. To make the bag stand, sew a straight line directly across the bottom seam about 1" from the end. Repeat for opposite ends. Turn right sides out. Topstitch around the top for a more professional look.

Tag

1. Cut a 3" x 4½" rectangle of yellow paper.
2. Attach vintage image near top of paper with pop dots. Insert a mini brad near each corner and tuck wispy trim under brads to form border.
3. Type or print "Congratulations" on white card stock to fit inside metal nameplate. Glue nameplate below vintage image.
4. Cut a 4½" x 10" rectangle of vellum. Fold over and sew on sides to create envelope. Insert tag.
5. Punch hole in upper-left corner of envelope. Thread ribbon through hole and loop in bag. Tie into bow.

Materials

- ¼" hole punch
- 1 yard decorator fabric
- 1 yard contrasting fabric
- 2 yards trim
- 4 mini brads
- Glue stick
- Metal nameplate
- Pop dots
- Ribbon
- Scissors
- Sewing machine
- Vellum
- Vintage image
- White card stock
- Wispy trim
- Yellow paper

And
when
that
rocket
ship
takes
ght,

Baby Suitcase

Box

1. Measure the bottom of the plastic case and cut the patterned paper to fit.
2. Arrange baby items in case and embellish with ribbons and charms.

Tag

1. Cut a square of patterned paper.
2. Type or print poem on slightly smaller piece of vellum.
3. Use the end of a brad to pierce two small holes in the top of the patterned paper. Thread through with a small piece of raffia.
4. Mount poem on patterned paper with brads.
5. Tie tag around bear's neck and add a ribbon.

Materials

- 4 star brads
- Baby items (T-shirts, baby blankets, bowls)
- Blue ribbon
- Blue vellum
- Organdy ribbon
- Patterned paper
- Plastic case
- Raffia
- Silver charms
- Teddy bear

A beautiful
treasure,
more precious
than gold,
your own
baby boy,
to love and
to hold.

Box

1. Paint box white. Let dry. Apply second coat. Let dry.
2. Stick felt letters on lower portion of lid to spell the words, "First Aid."
3. Cut out red cross and glue to center of box lid.

Tag

1. Add eyelet to corner of anatomy chart.
2. Tie string through eyelet. Secure other end of string to inside of box, using glue dot.
3. Conceal the glue dot with a circle punched from the red card stock.

Card

1. Cut a 4½" x 6½" rectangle from vellum. Fold sides and bottom back and secure with glue dots for envelope.
2. Glue envelope to lower front of box.
3. Type supply list and glue a red ribbon pull cord on the back. Mount on red card stock and place in envelope.

Materials

- ½" hole punch
- 17" white string or embroidery floss
- Card stocks: red and white
- Cardboard box
- Eyelet setter
- Felt alphabet stickers
- Glue dots
- Hammer
- Miniature anatomy chart
- Paintbrush
- Red ribbon
- Ruler
- Scissors
- Vellum
- White eyelets
- White paint

The Human Skeleton

supply list

band aids *alcohol wipes * aspirin *gauze*ace bandage * tape *scissors* cold compress

FIRST AID

Materials

- ¼" hole punch
- Card stocks: black and white
- Hair drier or embossing heat gun
- Iron
- Mini alphabet stamps
- Mini glue dots
- Mini scallop-edged scissors
- Organdy fabric
- Rhinestones
- Ribbon
- Ruler
- Sewing machine
- Silver embossing ink pad
- Silver embossing powder
- Small tooth fairy charm
- Small scissors
- Tooth-shaped punch
- Metal-rimmed vellum tag

Bag

1. Cut a 3" x 10" piece of organdy. Fold in 1½" on each short sides. Iron flat and sew edges down. Sew another seam ½" closer to fold to form casing.
2. Fold organdy in half, right side in. Sew long sides together. Turn right side out.
3. Using scissors, make a small vertical cut on each side of casing near the seams.
4. Cut the ribbon into two equal lengths. Thread one length of ribbon all the way through and back to where you started. Repeat with the remaining length of ribbon, starting on the opposite side. You should now have two ribbon ends at each side. Tie one pair in a knot and leave the other untied.

Tag

1. Punch hole in top of vellum tag. Thread with untied ribbon ends on bag and tie in a knot.
2. Attach tooth fairy charm to vellum tag with glue dot.

Card

1. Cut a 2¼" x 3¼" rectangle from black card stock. Fold over so that top part of card is about ½" shorter.
2. Trim bottom of card with scallop-edged scissors and attach rhinestones with mini glue dots.
3. Using mini alphabet stamps, stamp "believe" on top part of card.
4. Sprinkle embossing powder over letters. Shake off.
5. Heat with hair drier or embossing heat gun until powder beads up and turns shiny. Let dry.
6. Cut or punch tooth shape from white card stock. Glue above the word "believe."

Materials

- ¼" hole punch
- 8" twine
- Apple sticker
- Clear-drying craft glue
- Chalkboard spray paint
- Craft chalk
- Decorative chalkboard paper
- Glue dots
- Glue stick
- Plywood
- Ruler
- Sandpaper
- Scissors
- Small rectangular papier-mâché box
- Small wooden tag
- Waxed bag

Box

1. Cover the bottom half of box with decorative paper, using glue stick.
2. Apply chalkboard spray to a piece of plywood that is smaller than top of box. Let dry. Repeat.
3. Sand edges and surface.
4. Attach apple sticker on the bottom-right corner of the painted plywood.
5. Attach plywood to lid, using glue dots.

Tag

1. Spray wooden tag with chalkboard spray paint and let dry. Repeat.
2. Sand the edges for a more realistic look. Lightly sand the surface.
3. Using craft glue, attach 4" of twine to back of card. Tie a stick of chalk to remaining end of twine.
4. Cut decorative paper to fit the back of card and attach with glue stick.

Bag

1. Place a few pieces of colored chalk in waxed bag.
2. Fold over top and punch two holes with ¼" hole punch.
3. Thread twine through holes and knot in front.

Box

1. Carefully drill two small holes in top of plastic container. Fit with eyelets using eyelet setter and hammer.
2. Thread ribbon though eyelets for handle.
3. Using the awl, make four small holes for the nameplate in the front of the plastic container.
4. Fill with travel accessories.

Tag

1. Type or print a name for the nameplate on paper.
2. Cut to fit and attach the name and nameplate to plastic container, using the silver brads.

Card

1. Type or print greeting on paper.
2. Attach to tag with a star brad.

Materials

- 2 silver eyelets
- 4 small brads
- Awl
- Drill
- Eyelets
- Eyelet setter
- Grosgrain ribbon
- Hammer
- Paper
- Plastic container, large enough to hold travel accessories
- Scissors
- Silver nameplate
- Small star brad
- Square metal-rimmed tag
- Travel accessories (toothbrush holder, soap dish, shampoo bottles, etc.)

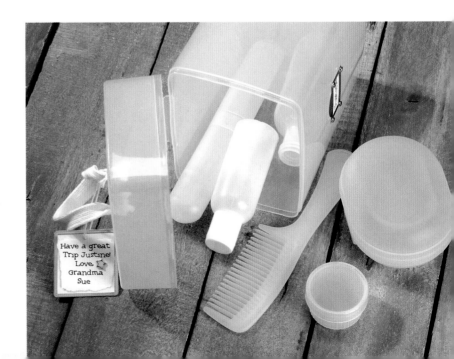

Ciao Bella

Materials

- ¼" hole punch
- Black fine-tipped marker
- Brown chalk
- Card stocks: red and white
- Crafting chalk
- Decorative paper with postage-stamp pattern
- Glue stick
- Ink pads: red, black, and brown
- Metal nameplate
- Mini brads
- Postage cancellation rubber stamps
- Red embroidery thread
- Ruler
- Scissors
- Small alphabet stamps
- Small cream-colored canvas tote bag

Bag

1. Randomly stamp canvas bag, using cancellation stamps and various colored inks.
2. Stamp "ciao bella" across border and sporadically on front of bag, using black or brown ink.

Tag

1. Cut tag out of red card stock. Cut 1" strip of decorative paper to match width of card. Tear off bottom edge and shade with brown chalk. Glue to top of tag.
2. Attach plaque to tag with brads.
3. Stamp "ciao bella" in plaque window with black ink.
4. Randomly stamp, using the cancellation stamps and various colored inks.
5. Punch hole in upper-left corner of tag with ¼" punch. Tie red embroidery thread through hole.

Card

1. Cut card from red card stock. Fold in half.
2. Cut 3½" x 1½" strip of white card stock. Punch a small circle in the top center with one-third of hole off edge.
3. Using marker, outline with three squiggly lines and shade with brown craft chalk.
4. Stamp "ticket" in lower-right corner, using black ink.
5. Cut a 3"-wide strip of decorative paper to match the height of card. Tear strip along the right side, then shade with brown chalk.
6. Place ticket underneath strip of paper, on an angle. Glue to left side of card.
7. Stamp "ciao bella" inside card, using black ink.
8. Randomly stamp decorative paper, using cancellation stamps and various colored inks.

Bon Voyage

Materials

- ¼" hole punch
- Black button
- Black embroidery floss
- Blue card stock
- Decorative paper with a map or travel pattern
- Glue dots
- Glue stick
- Ink pads: black and rust
- Metal CD box
- Paints: blue and white
- Plastic toy compass
- Sandpaper
- Scissors
- Small picture for tag
- Various-sized alphabet stamps

Box

1. Paint metal box with blue paint. Let dry.
2. Paint over blue paint with white acrylic paint. Let dry.
3. Scuff edges and top of box with sandpaper.
4. Stamp saying around edge of box, using black ink.
5. Attach compass, vintage images, and other objects on top of box as desired, using glue dots.

Tag

1. Cut out tag from card stock.
2. Cut and attach the small picture to the front of tag, using glue stick.
3. Stamp "life" under picture, using miniature alphabet stamps and black ink.
4. Punch ¼" hole for 9" embroidery floss. Fold in half and thread through hole for tag.

Card

1. Cut 12" x 2½" strip from blue card stock. Fold like an accordion, making each fold about 2", then press flat.
2. Select pictures in the decorative paper that represent a journey. Tear out and attach to the bottom of card, using glue stick.
3. Stamp desired saying in black ink, then restamp with with rust ink.
4. From the decorative paper, tear a picture that ties into the journey theme. Rub edges lightly with black ink pad and attach to front of card, using glue stick.
5. Glue small button to the right center of card front.
6. Fold card in accordion fashion. Wrap black thread around card and tuck under button.

TODAY IS THE FIRST DAY OF THE REST OF YOUR

LIFE

LIFE

Bon voyage

Materials

- ½" hole punch
- 1 yard red canvas strapping
- 2 metal-edged tags
- 2 mini brads
- 2 pencils
- 24" white string
- Ceramic charm alphabet stones to spell "car games"
- Decorative canvas towel
- Fabric glue
- Red felt alphabet stickers
- Red "X" and "O" stickers
- Sewing machine
- Straight pins
- Shoelaces
- Upholstery thread to match fabric
- White card stock
- White writing paper

Bag

1. Fold canvas towel in half, matching short ends together, and pin in place.
2. Sew up sides of bag, using matching upholstery thread.
3. Cut length of canvas strapping in half.
4. Secure canvas strappings with pins to form handles. Sew in place.
5. Hand-stitch ceramic letter stones on front of bag to spell "car games." (If no hole to secure by stitching, use fabric glue.)

Tags

1. Place the letter "O" sticker on oval or circle tag.
2. Place the letter "X" sticker on rectangular or square tag.
3. Tie and knot string through tag holes.
4. Push mini brad down center of pencil eraser, making sure string is between brad prongs before pushing down into eraser.

Card

1. Punch holes along left side of several sheets of paper and two sheets of card stock for front and back.
2. Thread shoelace through holes and tie each end in a knot to secure.
3. Stick felt letters on cover to spell out "TIC TAC TOE."

My Hero

Materials

- Alphabet stickers
- Card stocks: brown and yellow
- Clear varnish
- Empty Chinese take-out container
- Foam squares
- Glue stick
- Paintbrush
- Red polka-dot paper
- Red raffia
- Superhero comic strip
- Superhero stickers
- Waxed envelope

Box

1. Unfold Chinese take-out container and lay flat. Paint box with varnish, to act as an adhesive, then cover with superhero comic strip paper.
2. Put box back together and paint again with varnish to seal. Let dry.
3. Wrap red raffia around wire handle and tie ends. Cover with varnish and let dry.

Tag

1. Cut out square from comic strip of superhero.
2. Mount comic strip square on yellow card stock, then mount yellow card stock on brown card stock.
3. Mount brown card stock on the front of box, using foam squares.

Card

1. Cut the card from red polka-dot paper to fit the inside of waxed envelope.
2. Cut a piece of yellow card stock to fit front of card, using ⅛" border.
3. Add large stickers to spell "My Hero."
4. Add "S" emblem to front of waxed envelope.

Materials

- 3 star eyelets
- Black ink
- Brown embroidery floss
- Buttons
- Clothespins:
  1 miniature and
  1 full-sized
- Embroidery needle
- Eyelet setter
- Foam squares
- Gift bag
- Glue dots
- Glue gun
- Hammer
- Ruler
- Scissors
- Textured papers in coordinating patterns
- Various-sized alphabet stamps
- Zipper

Bag

1. Cut decorative paper to fit width and one half the height of gift bag. Tear along top edge.
2. Embroider an "X" on each corner of decorative paper. Attach to bag front with glue dots.
3. Glue on pieces of torn textured paper in a fashion that pleases you.
4. Add embroidery thread to button and attach to upper left-hand corner.
5. Add three star eyelets to upper left-hand corner.

Tag

1. Cut 3½" square from textured paper. Tear bottom.
2. Rub black ink on edges to give it a distressed look.
3. Stamp the words "Enjoy," using large and small letters.
4. Using glue gun, attach clothespin to top of tag.
5. Using foam squares, attach tag to bag.

Card

1. Fold paper to form card, leaving room for zipper.
2. Using embroidery floss, hand-stitch zipper onto paper, tucking bottom of zipper under back side of card. You will have to cut down the center of the back of the card to be able to sew the front all the way to the bottom.
3. Cover back with matching card stock to conceal.
4. Add button embellishments to front of card.
5. Blacken sides, using black ink on edges.
6. Make smaller tag, as described in Tag instructions above. Stamp the words "Have a."
7. Stamp "Happy Day" on inside of card.

Materials

- 1" square punch
- Card stocks: light pink, dark pink, and white
- Faux feathers: white and pink
- Faux-pearl decorative garland
- Glue dots
- Glue gun
- Glue stick
- Plastic "girlfriend" charm or alphabet stickers
- Small oval box
- Velcro
- White mini brad

Box

1. Using a glue stick, cover sides of box and top of lid with dark pink card stock.
2. Using a glue gun, attach pink faux feathers to the top and sides of lid.

Tag

1. Punch a 1" square from light pink card stock to form miniature purse.
2. Add string of faux pearls for handle, using glue dots.
3. Cut a triangle of white card stock for a purse flap. Use glue stick to apply to purse, covering the part where the handle is attached.
4. Cut head off white mini brad and apply head to bottom of triangle with glue stick.

Card

1. Cut a 5" x 11" strip of light pink card stock.
2. Fold over about 2" to form the purse flap, and fold the rest in half, tucking under flap.
3. Cut a 3" x 2" rectangle of dark pink paper and glue to a slightly larger rectangle of white paper.
4. Attach the "girlfriend" charm or alphabet stickers to the lower-left corner with glue dots.
5. Using glue dots, attach the white background to purse on an angle.
6. Using glue gun, attach white feathers to purse flap.
7. Using glue gun, add several strands of pearls to the upper-back corners of the purse to form the handle.
8. Cover with strip of pink card stock to hide glue.
9. Apply Velcro to inside of purse flap and corresponding point on the purse to keep it shut.

Light Up Your Life

Bag

1. Using dinner plate as a pattern, cut a circle of felt.
2. Fold the circle in half. Measure 1" down from the side just a little above the fold and punch one hole with the eyelet setter.
3. Repeat for the opposite side. Unfold the circle. You should now have four holes.
4. Fold the circle in other direction and repeat. Now you should have eight holes.
5. Using eyelet setter and hammer, add the eyelets.
6. Thread 1 yard of wide ribbon through the eyelets and pull tight.
7. Insert candle in bag and tie ribbon into bow.

Tag

1. Thread plastic-coated wire through beads to spell recipient's name. Glue to center of metal tag.
2. Wrap thin ribbon around bottom of tag and glue in place. Glue flower on top of ribbon.
3. Tie rickrack through hole in tag and tie onto bag.

Materials

- 8 eyelets
- Alphabet beads
- Cloth flower
- Eyelet setter
- Felt
- Glue gun
- Hammer
- Plastic-coated wire
- Ribbons: wide and narrow
- Rickrack
- Sewing machine
- Silk flowers, rickrack and trims
- Small metal tag

Chapter Two

Birthdays

What a Big Boy

Materials

- 2 small metal-rimmed vellum tags
- Black felt-tipped pen
- Black ink pad
- Card stocks: blue, white, and yellow
- Foam squares
- Fuzzy purple thread
- Glue dots
- Kite string
- Light blue bag
- Mini alphabet stamps
- Mini brads: 2 white star-shaped and 4 yellow
- Mini zigzag scissors
- Ruler
- Scissors

Bag

1. Make candle by cutting a 1½" x 5½" rectangle from white card stock. Tear flame shape from yellow card stock and attach to top with glue dot. Wrap and glue thread around candle.
2. Glue candle to bag.
3. Tear yellow strip and stamp "Happy Birthday." Attach with white star brads to bottom of candle, leaving small amount of candle peeking out from under strip.

Tag

1. Cut tag out of blue card stock. Trim bottom of tag with zigzag scissors. Outline with felt-tipped pen.
2. Make the candle, using a small rectangle of the white card stock.
3. Glue candle to tag on angle.
4. Stamp name on small, metal-rimmed vellum tag and attach to left side of tag with yellow brad.

Card

1. Cut card out of blue card stock. Fold in half and tear 1" from top layer to create a torn edge.
2. Make a smaller candle, as described in the bag instructions above.
3. Secure candle to center of card with foam squares.
4. Stamp "one" on metal-rimmed tag.
5. Thread string through tag and tie to purple thread.
6. Stamp "Happy Birthday to You" on front of card with mini alphabet stamps and black ink.
7. Stamp "What a Big Boy!" on yellow strip with mini alphabet stamps and black ink. Attach with yellow mini brads to bottom of card.

Birthday Bucket

Materials

- Colored brads
- Colored wire
- Glue stick
- Multicolored excelsior
- Patterned paper
- Red bucket
- Red mesh
- Rickrack
- Various dollar-store toys (bubbles, sidewalk chalk, ball, paddleball, jacks, foam star)
- Vellum

Container

1. Remove the label from the bubbles and glue a piece of patterned paper in its place.
2. Print or write "bubbles" on a strip of vellum and mount on a slightly larger strip of blue card stock.
3. Attach a colored brad at each end of label. Glue label to bubbles.
4. Wrap colored wire around one brad, then around back of bottle and around the other brad. Leave about 1" of wire to curl at the end of each brad.
5. Make similar labels for other items in the container.
6. Fill bucket with multicolored excelsior. Add toys and wrap bucket with red mesh.

Tag

1. Cut a tag from patterned paper.
2. Print "Happy Birthday" on strip of vellum and attach to tag with brads.
3. Twist two pieces of rickrack and attach to the back of the tag. Hang tag on the handle of bucket.

Happy B-day, Partner

Bag

1. Cut out denim paper rectangle.
2. Center on bag front and secure with glue stick.
3. Evenly space four rivet stickers on the bottom of the denim paper.
4. Use a red bandanna instead of tissue paper.

Tag

1. Attach pocket embellishment to tan card stock and glue together all edges, except top, to form a pocket.
2. Cut a 1" x 2" rectangle from tan card stock. On the top, stamp "To:" and "From:" Insert into pocket.
3. Glue twine to bag handle. Secure twine ends with glue and tuck ends under corners of pocket.

Card

1. Cut card out of tan card stock.
2. Attach denim picture border to front of card.
3. Add handkerchief sticker to top center of frame.
4. Add rivet sticker to each lower-inside corner of picture border.
5. Punch denim paper with small square punch. Stamp letters on denim squares to replace random letters in sentence.
6. Stamp birthday phrase.

Materials

- ½" square punch
- Brown ink pad
- Decorative denim paper
- Denim picture border
- Denim pocket embellishment
- Gift bag
- Glue stick
- Handkerchief stickers
- Red bandanna
- Rivet stickers
- Ruler
- Scissors
- Small alphabet stamps
- Tan card stock
- Twine

To:
From:

HAPPY
BIRTH-
DAY
partner

Materials

- ¼" hole punch
- Black ink pad
- Brown shipping tag
- Card stocks: brown and purple
- Craft glue
- Glue dots
- Mini alphabet stamps
- Mini faux pearls
- Mini gold brads
- Ruler
- Scissors
- Small brown paper bag
- Twine
- Vellum scrap

Bag

1. Cut a 2" strip of purple card stock to fit across front of bag, and attach with glue dots.
2. Stamp message on front under purple strip with alphabet stamps.
3. Make two pansies from torn circles of purple card stock and attach in centers with gold brads.
4. Attach pansies above purple strip with glue dots.
5. Make birthday cake from torn paper and vellum.
6. Tear purple paper to form candles.
7. Attach pearls for candle flames, using craft glue.

Tag

1. Make two pansies and attach with glue dots to bottom of brown shipping tag.
2. Stamp "Happy Birthday to You" on front.
3. Cut a 1" square of purple card stock. Glue over hole in shipping tag. Punch through paper and existing hole.
4. Tie twine through hole.

Card

1. Cut a 3½" x 2½" rectangle of brown card stock.
2. Cut a 3" length of twine and form into a loop, attaching to top of tag with glue dots.
3. Cut a strip of purple card stock to fit top of card, and tear off the bottom to create torn edge. Use craft glue to attach to top of square, covering glue dots.
4. Stamp birthday message on front of card.
5. Fashion envelope from small brown paper bag by folding edges in back and securing with glue dots.
6. Make two pansies and attach to front of envelope, using craft glue.

Birthday Candles

Materials

- 1½" square punch
- 2½" box
- Alphabet stickers
- Candles: 3 pink and 2 yellow
- Decorative papers: light green and mulberry
- Glue dots
- Glue stick
- Lollipops or candy
- Pink chenille thread
- Pink mini brads
- Ruler
- Scissors
- Shipping tag
- Shredded paper
- Small square of plastic foam
- Vellum

Box

1. Line inside of box with mulberry paper.
2. Wrap light green paper around box, leaving small border of mulberry.
3. Cut vellum square slightly smaller than front of box. Attach with pink mini brads.
4. Wrap pink candle in pink chenille thread. Attach to center of vellum with glue dots.
5. Cut plastic foam to fit in bottom of box.
6. Fill box with shredded paper and lollipops.

Tag

1. Cut out light green decorative paper to match size of shipping tag. Adhere paper to tag with glue stick.
2. Using glue dots, attach one yellow and one pink candle to center of tag.
3. Cut vellum to fit bottom half of tag, covering bottom half of candles.
4. Attach pink brads around edges.
5. Glue pink thread to top of vellum.
6. String pink thread through hole in tag.

Card

1. Cut card from light green decorative paper. Fold in half.
2. Using sticker letters, spell out "Birthday" on card top.
3. Punch square in lower-right corner of card.
4. Glue pink thread across center of card.
5. Attach pink brads in corners of square.
6. Cut one pink and one yellow candle to 1" and attach in window of card with glue dots.

Materials

- 2 white slide frames
- Alphabet stickers
- Black marker
- Blue colored pencil
- Buttons
- Card stocks: dark purple and yellow
- Dark purple bag
- Glue dots
- Metal-rimmed tag
- Multicolored string
- Rickrack in two contrasting colors
- Stickers

Bag

1. Cut two strips of rickrack in contrasting colors to fit width of bag. Attach to bottom of bag with glue dots, overlapping slightly.
2. Attach buttons over rickrack with glue dots.

Tag

1. Place white slide cover on back of tag. Inside slide frame, write the name of the recipient with black marker. Let dry.
2. Shade with blue colored pencil.
3. Decorate reverse side of tag with stickers if desired.

Card

1. Cut card from dark purple card stock. Fold in half.
2. Arrange alphabet stickers to cover card front and spell the word "Sweet."
3. Cut yellow card stock to fit slide. Glue inside slide.
4. Handwrite "16." Let dry.
5. Shade with blue colored pencil.
6. Add white slide cover for definition.
7. Wrap with multicolored string.
8. Add movie tickets, gift certificates, or even cash inside card or under string.
9. Use stickers to spell "Happy Birthday" inside card.

Bag

1. Punch circles from all the colors of card stock. Glue circles and rickrack to full sheet of white card stock.
2. Roll decorated card stock into a tube shape and seal edge with glue stick.
3. Fill tube with shredded paper and gift or candy.
4. Wrap tube in cellophane and tie ends with ribbon.

Tag

1. Cut the tag from pink card stock.
2. Using the hole punch, create confetti from the pink, yellow, and blue card stocks.
3. Sew two small pieces of cellophane together to make a tiny bag.
4. Place the confetti in the small bag and tie with ribbon.
5. Using eyelet setter and hammer, set the heart eyelet in the tag hole.
6. Cut a strip of card stock to fit width of tag. Type or print the word "Celebrate" and glue to tag.
7. Attach rickrack and party bag to tag with glue stick.
8. Glue tag to package.

Materials

- ¼" hole punch
- Blue rickrack
- Candy or gift
- Card stocks: white, pink, blue, and yellow
- Cellophane
- Circle punch
- Eyelet setter
- Glue stick
- Hammer
- Heart eyelet
- Ribbon
- Scissors
- Sewing machine
- Shredded paper

A Present for You

Materials

- 1 blue brad
- 2 silver mini brads
- Alphabet stamps
- Card stocks: white and blue
- Felt: blue, red, yellow, and green
- Glue gun
- Glue stick
- Large button
- Needle and thread
- Paper candles
- Rickrack
- Scissors
- Scrap of vellum

Bag

1. Cut two pieces of felt and sew together on three sides.
2. Fold down top 1" of bag. Wrap thin rickrack around outside of bag.
3. Sew large button to front of bag, over the rickrack.
4. Cut a piece of red felt about 1" square. Cut a piece of yellow felt about ¾" square and glue over red square.
5. Cut two thin strips of green felt and glue them over yellow and red squares in a crisscross pattern, tucking ends under red square.
6. Glue red "present" to center of bag.
7. Cut green felt in the shape of a bow and attach to bag above present, using blue brad.

Tag

1. Cut the white card stock to the desired tag size.
2. Tear a small piece of the blue card stock.
3. Attach the two candles over the blue card stock.
4. Stamp name of the recipient on vellum and attach with mini brads.

Materials

- 4 copper brads
- Alphabet stamps
- Bone folder
- Button
- Corrugated paper
- Glue gun or craft glue
- Kraft card stock
- Oil or chalk pastels
- Raffia
- Small watercolor tablet
- Small wood easel
- Vellum

Gift Idea

1. Cut a piece of the kraft card stock the same size as the oil pastel box. Wrap around box and glue at seam.
2. Using the bone folder, make creases along edges.
3. Slide this piece of paper over the box.
4. Cut a piece of corrugated paper about 2" narrower than the width of the box. Wrap around center of box, using bone folder, and glue in place.
5. Using the alphabet stamps, stamp "Pastels" on the corrugated paper.
6. Place the pastel box on the easel and secure with a small amount of glue.
7. Place the watercolor tablet on top of the pastel box and secure with a small amount of glue.
8. Tie a raffia ribbon around easel, over boxes, and attach the button.

Card

1. Cut an 8" x 4½" rectangle from kraft card stock.
2. Fold kraft card stock in half, using bone folder.
3. Tear a piece of the corrugated brown paper to accent the front. Trim to fit and attach to card with glue.
4. Place a small piece of raffia down the middle of the corrugated paper. Glue to secure.
5. Type or print message on a piece of vellum. Cut vellum to fit and attach to card with brads.

Bath Salt

Materials

- Alphabet impression stamps
- Alphabet stickers
- Bath salt
- Drill
- Floral stickers
- Flower-shaped metal tag
- Glue gun
- Hammer
- Organdy ribbon
- Patterned papers in contrasting prints
- Scissors
- Small paint can
- Small wooden spoon
- White card stock

Can

1. Measure the can and cut the patterned paper to fit. Attach paper with glue gun.
2. Tear a strip of contrasting-print paper about 3" wide and glue over the paper seam.
3. Cut a strip of white card stock for a label, and attach alphabet stickers to form the word "Bath."
4. Glue label to can and decorate with stickers.
5. Carefully drill a small hole in the top of the can.
6. Thread the organdy ribbon through the hole and tie a knot to secure, forming a handle.
7. Thread a piece of silk ribbon through the wooden spoon. Glue ribbon just inside of the can.
8. Fill can with bath salt.

Tag

1. Hammer the word "salt" onto the metal tag using impression stamps.
2. Tie a ribbon through tag and attach to front of can.

Spa-cial Birthday

Basket

1. Place the excelsior in the basket.
2. Place the spa products in the basket.
3. For seashell with sea salts, wash and dry shell thoroughly. Place salt inside and cover with cellophane.
4. String the garland over the basket.

Tag

1. Working very slowly and with a small drill bit, drill a small hole at the top of the shell.
2. Glue on raffia, greeting, vellum, and charm. Attach to basket with raffia.

Materials

- Cellophane
- Charms or other embellishments
- Drill
- Excelsior
- Glue gun
- Large seashell for the sea salt
- Raffia
- Sea salt
- Seashell or other embellished garland
- Small flat seashell for the tag
- Spa products (scrub brush, pumice stone, soap, soap holder, wash cloth)
- Vellum for the tag
- Wood basket

Blooming Good Day

Materials

- Angel charm
- Bulb flower-growing kit (Amaryllis, Paper White, Calla Lily, etc.)
- Burlap
- Cream card stock
- Floral die-cuts
- Floral patterned paper
- Glue gun
- Gold nameplate
- Gold ribbon
- Green tissue paper
- Large plastic vase
- Photo corners
- Pop dots
- Scissors
- Soil
- Wide silk ribbon

Container

1. Remove flower kit from its box. Place the pot from kit inside the large vase. Place bulb inside pot.
2. Fill burlap with soil and tie shut, using raffia.
3. Strategically place the green tissue paper around top of vase. Place burlap bag inside vase.
4. Wrap ribbon over the top of the vase and place a small dollop of glue at the bottom to secure.
5. Tie ribbon, and glue angel charm to the knot.

Tag

1. Type or print text on cream card stock, small enough to center inside nameplate. Trim to fit.
2. Attach card stock to nameplate with glue.
3. Attach the nameplate to the front of the vase with glue.

Card

1. Type or print the growing instructions from the flower kit onto a square of cream card stock.
2. Mount on a slightly larger square of patterned paper, using photo corners, leaving a few inches of extra space at the top.
3. Attach the die-cuts on the patterned paper above the instructions, using pop dots.
4. Punch two holes in the top of the patterned paper. Thread through with gold ribbon.

Calla Lily
(Aethiopica)

- Soak the potting mix well, squeezing out any excess water.

- Plant the bulb round side down, 1" below surface of potting mix.

- Place in a bright, sunny spot. (Indirect sunlight is best.)

- Keep the soil moist at all times.

- After lily blooms, plant in garden.

Calla Lily
(Aethiopica)

Materials

- Card stock
- Cigar box
- Decoupage medium
- Die-cuts
- Glue gun
- Hammer
- Mesh ribbon
- Patterned paper
- Picture or drawing that complements the patterned paper
- Pop dots
- Rag
- Scissors
- Upholstery nails

Box

1. Remove all stickers from cigar box.
2. Cut strips of patterned paper to go around all four sides of box and apply with decoupage medium, working quickly.
3. Cut a square of patterned paper slightly smaller than the top of the box. Tear off right side and decoupage to top of box.
4. Decoupage picture to center of patterned paper on the box top.
5. Using a hammer, gently tap the upholstery nails into the desired location.
6. Secure ribbon in place, using the glue gun.
7. Take a damp rag and gently rub over patterned paper to create a distressed look.
8. Place the die-cuts on top of the ribbon, using pop dots.
9. If desired, the inside of the box may be embellished in the same manner.

Tag

1. Type or print a poem on a square of card stock.
2. Attach over ribbon with glue gun.

Rosa Ventenatiana.   Rosier Ventenat.

P.J. Redouté pinx.   Imprimerie de Rémond.

You were made perfectly to be loved
and surely I have loved you,
in the idea of you,
my whole life long.

Elizabeth Barrett Browning

Materials

- 3-D clear craft glue
- Clock sticker
- Coffee or tea
- Cotton swab
- Flat dish
- Gift bag
- Glue stick
- Ink pads: black and brown
- Kite string
- Manila tag
- Miniature alphabet/ number stamps
- Old cloth
- Ruler
- Scissors
- Small lid to metal container with clear cover
- Tan card stock
- Tea bag
- Two styles decorative paper
- Watch parts

Bag

1. Tear edges of decorative paper and glue to all sides of the bottom half of the bag.
2. Place clock sticker on right side of bag.

Tag

1. Soak tag and string in flat dish filled with hot black coffee or tea for several minutes. Set wet tea bag on different parts of tag to create an aged, stained look. Let dry. Tie string to tag.
2. Using clear craft glue, apply small amount to bottom of tag with cotton swab. Place small watch parts across top of glue strip. Let dry.
3. Lightly mark spot under lid where numbers will be, then stamp numbers with brown ink.
4. Using clear craft glue, add watch parts to reflect center piece and watch hands. Let dry.
5. Apply craft glue to underside of lid and place over top of clock face. Let dry. Tie string through hole.

Card

1. Cut card from card stock. Fold in half.
2. Tear decorative paper diagonally and glue to card.
3. Glue another piece of decorative paper to inside of card with glue stick. Let dry.
4. Fold card on crease. Insert doubled old cloth to prevent tea water from bleeding through.
5. Dip tea bag in coffee, then use to "paint" entire card face. Let bag sit for several minutes in different spots to create aged, stained areas.
6. Once dry, you may need to reglue torn paper around edges. Work paper back into smooth, presentable card, using iron if necessary.
7. Using black ink, stamp sayings on front and inside.

Chapter Three

Seasonal

happy holidays

Nasturtia
Crystals

MOM

Materials

- Black thread
- Card stocks: red and brown
- Jewelry tag
- Mini glue dots
- Mini red heart candies
- Primitive heart punch
- Red ink pad
- Red raffia scrap
- Small, sealable plastic bag

Bag

1. Fill plastic bag with candies, then seal.
2. Cut a square of brown card stock to fit width of bag. Fold over top of bag and secure with mini glue dots.
3. Cut three primitive hearts from red card stock and glue to front of brown card stock.

Tag

1. Cut a small primitive heart from red card stock and glue to jewelry tag.
2. Tie black thread through hole in jewelry tag. Wrap thread around a heart on bag top and secure with mini glue dot.

Card

1. Cut a 3" square of brown card stock. Fold over in half.
2. Glue strip of red raffia horizontally in center of card.
3. Cut two primitive hearts from red construction paper and glue over raffia.

For My Daughter

Bag

1. Cut felt to fit gift, leaving a 1" seam allowance on the sides and bottom and an extra piece on the top to fold over as a flap.
2. Sew sides together.
3. Fold and sew flap to create triangle.
4. Decorate envelope with embellished ribbon and vintage buttons.

Tag

1. Type or print message on vellum.
2. Sew ribbon around edges of tag, stringing a pearl onto the ribbon in between each stitch.

Materials

- Embellished ribbon
- Green silk ribbon
- Needle
- Pearl beads
- Pink felt
- Scissors
- Sewing machine
- Vellum
- Vintage buttons

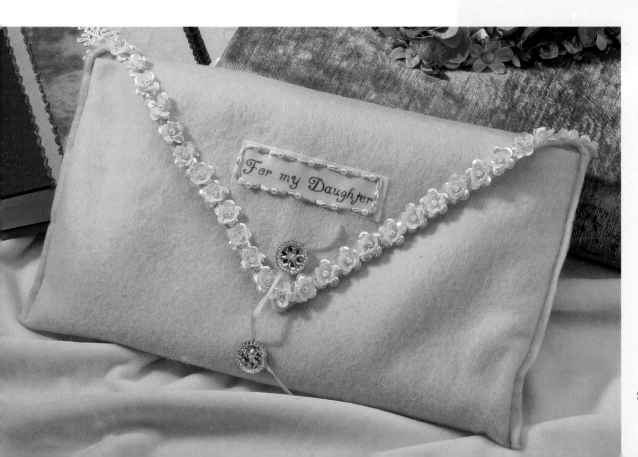

Box

1. Paint top of mint tin with black paint. Let dry.
2. Paint heart in center of tin, using craft glue.
3. Add beads and fill in with microbeads. Let dry.
4. Type or print a definition of "love" on white card stock. Cut to fit box top and attach with craft glue. Dab with pink ink pad.

Tag

1. Smear caulk on front of wooden tag. Let dry.
2. Paint black. Let dry.
3. Rub gently with sandpaper.
4. Thread needle and string two strands of beads, each several inches long. Tie one through the hole in the tag for a hanger. Attach the other to the bottom of the tag, using glue dots, as an embellishment.
5. Type or print a definition of "love" on white card stock. Attach diagonally to tag with craft glue and trim off any overhanging edges.
6. Attach silver key to front of tag with glue dot.

Card

1. Cut a card from pink card stock. Fold over in half and paint cover black, leaving pink patches. Let dry.
2. Type or print a definition of "eternal" on white card stock and attach to card front with craft glue.
3. Thread a strand of silver beads and attach to bottom of card front, securing to inside of card with glue dots.
4. Cover inside of card with pink floral paper, attaching with craft glue.

Materials

- ½" hole punch
- Black acrylic paint
- Card stocks: pink and white
- Caulking
- Craft glue
- Glue dots
- Mint tin
- Needle
- Paintbrush
- Pink floral paper
- Pink ink pad
- Sandpaper
- Scissors
- Silver beads
- Silver key
- Silver micro beads
- Thread
- Wooden tag

ETERNAL

1. without beginning or end; everlasting
2. neverchanging
3. **NEVER STOPPING**
4. something timeless, uninterrupted

love (luv) a strong, deep, affection and devotion

love (luv) a strong, deep, affection and devotion for another, unconditional and unexplained

Materials

- ¹⁄₁₆" hole punch
- ¼" hole punch
- Black felt-tipped pen
- Brown chalk
- Brown wire
- Card stocks: light brown, dark brown, and pink
- Glue gun
- Glue stick
- Large balloon punch
- Light brown gingham decorative paper
- Pink bunny sticker
- Pink Easter basket grass
- Pink mini alphabet stickers
- Pink mini paper bag
- Pink plaid wire-edged ribbon, 1½" wide and 9" long
- Scissors: regular and mini scallop-edged
- Small pink bow
- Twine

Bag / Tag

1. Cut tag from dark brown card stock.
2. Trim bottom with scallop-edged scissors and punch a ¹⁄₁₆" hole in each scallop.
3. Outline tag with black felt-tipped pen.
4. Punch ¼" hole in top of tag. Tie twine through hole. Fray edges of twine.
5. Use balloon punch to punch balloon shape from pink card stock. Turn upside down and draw bunny face with felt-tipped pen. Attach to tag with glue stick.
6. Curl wire and hot-glue under the bunny's nose to form whiskers. Chalk around edges.
7. Tear ears from pink card stock. Dust with brown chalk and glue to bunny face.
8. Attach small pink bow between ears with glue gun.
9. Tear ears from brown card stock. Chalk edges and attach to upper-back side of bag with glue stick.
10. Fill bag with Easter basket grass.
11. Attach tag to front of bag with glue stick.

Card

1. Cut card from light brown card stock and fold in half.
2. Glue decorative paper on inside, folding over to cover 1" of top of card.
3. Using mini scallop-edged scissors, cut square from light brown card stock. Punch ¹⁄₁₆" hole in each scallop to make it look like lace, and attach pink mini alphabet stickers to spell "Happy Easter."
4. Mount square on pink card stock. Trim edges with scallop-edged scissors and glue to card.
5. Punch two ¼" holes in top of card, ½" from sides.
6. Thread ribbon through holes and knot.
7. Apply bunny sticker to inside of card.

Materials

- ¼" hole punch
- 1" square punch
- Card stocks: yellow and moss green
- Craft glue
- Floral decorative paper
- Large alphabet stamps
- Pink ink pad
- Pink wire-edged ribbon
- Small vellum envelopes
- Thin pink ribbon

Bag

1. Cut a 12" square of decorative paper and fold-in three corners to center.
2. Secure by gluing a 1" square of moss green card stock over the point where the three corners meet. Glue a slightly smaller square of decorative paper over the green card stock.
3. Glue yellow card stock to the inside of envelope.
4. Secure wire ribbon with glue dots to form handle.

Tag

1. Cut a tag from yellow card stock. Punch two ¼" holes near the top. Tie thin pink ribbon through holes and into a bow.
2. Cut out decorative emblems from paper or use stickers that coordinate with cover of card.
3. Stamp "MOM" on tag, using pink ink.
4. Lightly rub edges of tag against pink ink pad.

Card

1. Layer a sheet of decorative paper and a sheet of yellow card stock. Cut into 5" x 4½" pieces.
2. Insert vellum envelopes between squares, with decorative side of decorative paper facing outward.
3. Punch two holes near the left edge of the stack of papers, and tie them together with wire-edged ribbon.
4. Place pictures of family or poems in envelopes.

Materials

- 2" hole punch
- 8 eyelets
- Alphabet stamps
- Decorative paper
- Eyelet punch
- Eyelet setter
- Fabric scraps in contrasting colors
- Glue gun
- Glue stick
- Green ink pad
- Hammer
- Iron
- Large dinner plate
- Ribbon
- Round metal tag
- Scissors
- Sewing machine
- Silk flowers

Bag

1. Using dinner plate as a pattern, cut two circles of fabric in contrasting colors.
2. Sew the two pieces together, right sides in, leaving a small opening for turning. Turn right sides out and press the seams. Topstitch all around, making sure to close the opening.
3. Fold the circle in half. Measure 1" down from the side just a little above the fold and hammer a hole with the eyelet punch.
4. Do the same at the opposite side. Unfold the circle. You should now have four holes.
5. Fold the circle again and do the same. Now you have eight holes.
6. Using eyelet setter and hammer, add the eyelets.
7. Cut two lengths of ribbon. Thread through eyelets at opposite sides and pull tightly.
8. Add potpourri and tie off.
9. Glue on a silk flower or other embellishment.

Tag

1. Cut a piece of decorative paper in the shape of the metal tag. Stamp the word "Mom" across the paper with alphabet stamps.
2. Attach paper to metal tag.
3. Tie onto bag with ribbon.

Mother's Garden

Materials

- ⅛" hole punch
- 1" square punch
- 2 seed packets
- 3" vellum strip torn approximately 1" wide
- 4" x 8" cellophane bag
- Alphabet stamps
- Black ink pad
- Candy
- Clear craft glue
- Fabric or paper flower
- Glue dot
- Green card stock
- Moss green card stock
- Ruler
- Safety pin
- Scissors
- Silk leaves
- Small flour sack
- Stickers: small flower and garden shovel
- Twine
- Yellow handmade paper

Bag

1. Stamp the word "Mother" on bottom of flour sack.
2. Place a small piece of card stock between the layers of the bag to prevent glue from sticking to bottom layer. Attach fabric or paper flower to bottom corner of bag.
3. Fill bag with Mom's favorite candy or treat.

Tag

1. Cut a small tag from green card stock.
2. Attach shovel sticker in center.
3. Secure vellum strip to bottom with glue dots.
4. Punch hole in top center. Tie twine through hole.

Card

1. Place two seed packets inside of cellophane bag.
2. Secure top of bag with twine, inserting silk leaf in knot.
3. Cut a square of green card stock. Attach small flower sticker to center of square. Glue square to a scrap of yellow, hand-torn paper.
4. Tie another piece of twine around middle of bag.
5. Glue paper square over top of knot.

Materials

- 1" x 1" image of your father
- 1" x 1" image of yourself as a child
- ¾" hole punch
- Black embroidery floss
- Black ink pad
- Black photo corners
- Brown chalk
- Card stocks: light brown, rusty brown, and dark brown
- Cotton swabs
- Glue gun
- Glue stick
- Manila tag
- Mini alphabet stamps
- Ruler
- Rust-colored mini brads
- Scissors
- Scrabble letters
- Small cardboard gift box
- Twine

Box

1. Lightly press black ink pad against all sides of box.
2. Wrap twine around box and tie bow on top.

Tag

1. Apply brown chalk to the edges of the tag. Blend with a cotton swab or makeup sponge.
2. Mount image of your father on dark brown card stock, then light brown, and then dark brown again, for a layered effect. Glue on bottom of tag.
3. Using a glue gun, attach Scrabble letters above picture to spell out "Dad."
4. Above the word "Dad," gently wrap twine around several times and tie a knot.
5. Thread 8½" of twine through hole and attach to bag.

Card

1. Cut a 7⅛" x 2¾" rectangle from rusty brown card stock.
2. Fold over, leaving bottom half about ½" longer.
3. Lightly press face of ink pad onto card front and let dry. You may want to practice on scrap paper.
4. Secure two circles punched from dark brown card stock to center of card stock on open meeting edges of card. Place mini brads in center of holes. Tie black embroidery floss around one of the brads on the cover.
5. Using alphabet stamps and black ink, stamp "father" on front center and "friend" on right corner.
6. Cut dark brown card stock to form inside of card. Cut it slightly smaller than the card to leave a border.
7. Use photo corners to place image of yourself on inside cover of card. Write a short message inside card.

Patriotic Box

Box

1. Remove handle from box.
2. Paint the box the desired color. Let dry.
3. Add photo corners to photo and glue to front of box.
4. Glue the wire garland around bottom and top of box.
5. Thread ribbon and a small piece of the garland through the holes in the top of box where handles used to be.

Materials

- Acrylic paint
- Copy of a vintage photograph
- Craft glue
- Glue gun
- Paint
- Paintbrush
- Photo corners
- Ribbon
- Wire garland
- Wooden "sack type" box with handle

Halloween Greeting

Bag

1. Cut felt in half to create two 5½" x 8½" pieces. Set aside.
2. Remove backing from iron-on stabilizer and iron onto 8½" x 11" piece of muslin, following manufacturer's instructions.
3. Scan an image and print it onto stabilized muslin sheet as you would with a regular piece of paper.
4. Trim image and iron-on bonding adhesive to a little smaller than bag front. Remove backing from adhesive and iron onto back of image. Remove second backing and iron onto the bag front.
5. Hand-stitch around image.
6. Sew felt pieces together along sides and bottom, with right sides in. Sew a straight seam on each corner of the bottom seam, about ½" in.
7. Turn bag right side out and fold top edge down.

Tag

1. Create words by stamping tag with impression stamps and gluing on alphabet beads.
2. Attach to bag with raffia and glue.

Materials

- ¼ yard high-quality muslin fabric
- 8½" x 11" piece of felt
- Alphabet beads
- Computer, scanner, ink-jet printer
- Copper tag
- Glue gun
- Iron
- Iron-on bonding adhesive
- Iron-on stabilizer for ink-jet printers
- Photograph or image
- Raffia string
- Sewing machine
- Tool impression stamps

Materials

- ¼" hole punch
- Card stocks: brown and yellow
- Glue dots
- Green thread
- Orange vellum
- Ribbon
- Ruler
- Scissors
- Small jewelry box
- Small paper leaves
- Twine

Box

1. Tie ribbon around box.
2. Attach green thread to stem of a paper leaf and attach to box top with glue dot. Glue other end of thread under ribbon.
3. Layer a second leaf over first, using glue dot.

Tag

1. Cut out tag from brown card stock.
2. Glue 1½" yellow strip to bottom of tag.
3. Glue 1" orange vellum strip over yellow strip.
4. Glue leaves to tag to look as if they are falling.
5. Cut approximately ¾" yellow square and slightly smaller orange vellum square and glue to top center of tag.
6. Punch hole in center of squares. Loop twine through hole and tie.

Card

1. Cut a 7½" square of orange vellum. Fold in three corners to center to create envelope. Cut off fourth corner.
2. Cut brown card stock to fit inside envelope.
3. Cut 1½" square from brown card stock and mount on slightly larger yellow card stock background.
4. Glue to center of envelope.
5. Glue leaf onto center of square.

Itsy Bitsy Spider

Box

1. Using a sharp knife, cut out face from lid of box.
2. Paint box and lid black. Let dry.
3. Using sponge, dab white paint around mouth and eyes of face. Let dry.
4. Paint stars around lip of lid. Let dry.
5. Lightly sand edges of box and lid to give aged look.
6. Using glue dots, attach mesh to inside of lid. Trim excess mesh.

Tag

1. Cut out tag from orange card stock.
2. Shape bottom of tag with decorative scissors.
3. Attach spider to front of tag with foam square.
4. For string, use black embroidery thread.
5. Stamp "booooooo" across bottom of tag.

Card

1. Cut card out of orange card stock.
2. Fold card in half.
3. Cut opening end with decorative scissors.
4. Using foam squares, attach spiders to opening edge of card, about ½" from edge.
5. Glue black thread from top of card to second spider.
6. Stamp "Halloween" on bottom of card.

Materials

- 7½"-diameter papier-mâché box
- Acrylic paints: black and oyster white
- Black embroidery floss
- Black ink pad
- Black spiders
- Decorative scissors
- Foam squares
- Glue dots
- Mini alphabet stamps
- Orange card stock
- Paintbrush
- Sandpaper
- Sharp knife
- Silver mesh
- Sponge

Materials

- 1" square punch
- 2 large gold safety pins
- Black felt-tipped pen
- Brown chalk
- Brown embroidery floss
- Brown florist's wire
- Brown ink pad
- Brush
- Card stocks: orange and tan
- Craft glue
- Fabric tape
- Foam squares
- Glue dots
- Gold glitter
- Gold pumpkin charm
- Mini buttons: black and orange
- Miniature shoe buckle
- Papier-mâché box
- Pencil
- Raffia
- Ribbon
- Ruler
- Scissors
- Thin ribbon
- Vellum

Box

1. Rub brown ink over box edges. Add stitches with pen.
2. Tear pumpkin shape from card stock. Chalk edges. Mark stitches with pen.
3. String raffia through buckle and attach to pumpkin with foam square. Glue raffia under pumpkin with glue dots.
4. Wrap florist's wire around pencil to curl. Brush on a light coat of craft glue and sprinkle with gold glitter. Let dry. Glue to pumpkin box top.
5. Glue strands of raffia horizontally above pumpkin.
6. Glue raffia partially under right side of pumpkin.
7. Loop and pin a 4" strip of fabric tape to pumpkin top with large gold safety pin. Glue three orange buttons to right side of fabric.
8. Glue loop to top of pumpkin.

Tag

1. Cut tag from tan card stock. Chalk edges. Mark stitches.
2. Print "Happy Halloween" in small letters on small strip of vellum. Glue on decorative mini buttons.
3. Loop fabric tape as described in box instructions. Add a pumpkin charm to pin and glue or pin to top of tag.
4. Tear paper scraps from orange card stock and glue together for pumpkin. Chalk edges and mark stitches.
5. Curl embroidery floss and glue to pumpkin stem.
6. Loop ribbon through fabric to create tag attachment.

Card

1. Cut card from orange card stock. Fold in half.
2. Punch two squares from tan card stock. Cut in half diagonally and glue to corners of card front. Chalk edges. Mark stitches.
3. Print "Happy Halloween" on vellum and glue to card.
4. Glue raffia on left side of vellum. Glue on buttons.

happy Halloween

Happy
Halloween

Best Xmas Wishes

Materials

- ¼ yard high-quality muslin fabric
- 8½" x 11" felt
- Button
- Computer, scanner, ink-jet printer
- Glue gun
- Iron-on bonding adhesive
- Iron
- Iron-on stabilizer for ink-jet printers
- Photograph or image
- Ribbon
- Rickrack
- Sewing machine

Bag

1. Cut felt in half so that you have two 5½" x 8½" pieces. Set aside.
2. Remove backing from iron-on stabilizer and iron onto 8½" x 11" piece of muslin, following manufacturer's instructions.
3. Scan the image you want to print. Print image onto the stabilized muslin sheet, just as you would a regular sheet of paper.
4. Trim image to a little smaller than bag front. Trim iron-on bonding adhesive to size of image. Remove backing and iron onto back of image. Remove second backing and iron onto the bag front.
5. Sew rickrack around image.
6. Place both pieces of felt, right sides together, and sew along sides and bottom. To make the bag stand, sew a straight seam on each corner of the bottom seam, about ½" in. Turn right sides out.
7. Punch three holes along top of bag in front and back. Thread ribbon through holes, tie bow, and add button.

Materials

- 1 yellow felt scrap
- 2 blue felt squares
- 2 colored brads
- 21" piece of rickrack
- Embroidery flosses: red and white
- Large button
- Needle
- Small alphabet stamps
- Vellum scrap

Bag

1. Cut two mittens from the blue felt, following pattern.
2. Stitch greeting to top mitten (thumb facing left).
3. Cut a star from the yellow felt scrap.
4. Sew the star below the greeting with a primitive stitch.
5. Tear a small strip of vellum and stamp with greeting.
6. Attach vellum over star, using the two brads.
7. Sew the two mittens, wrong sides together.
8. Sew the rickrack to the mitten, starting at the top right, and going all the way around, making a handle.
9. Sew on the button at the top right, where the two sides of the rickrack meet.

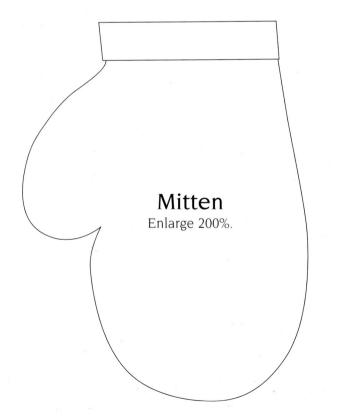

Mitten
Enlarge 200%.

Materials

- ¼" circle punch
- ½" circle punch
- ¾" square punch
- 1½" square punch
- 2 yards of chocolate-colored ribbon
- 2½" x 4¾" shipping tag
- Brown ink pad
- Card stocks: cream, dark brown, and mustard yellow
- Chocolate-chip print paper
- Coffee mug stickers
- Craft glue
- Glue dots
- Glue stick
- Foam square
- Heavy cream-colored yarn
- Hot chocolate recipe
- Scissors
- Small bag
- Various styles and sizes of rubber alphabet stamps
- White typing paper

Bag

1. Cover bottom third of bag with chocolate-chip print paper, using glue stick.
2. Punch ¾" square out of dark brown card stock and attach coffee mug sticker in center.
3. Attach card stock square to lower-right corner of bag with foam square.
4. Using craft glue, attach yarn in wavy lines for "steam."
5. Punch two holes in top of bag and thread with ribbon.

Tag

1. Cut a tag shape from yellow card stock.
2. Punch a hole in top and add reinforcements to sides.
3. Print out recipe for hot chocolate on white paper, making certain it is not wider than tag.
4. Tear around edges of recipe and glue to front of tag.
5. Punch three ½" circles from dark brown card stock and glue to bottom of tag.
6. Tie chocolate-colored ribbon through hole in tag.

Card

1. Cut a 5" x 8" card from dark brown card stock.
2. Fold up from bottom, leaving 1" at top to fold down.
3. Cut a 4½" x 3" piece of mustard yellow card stock and secure with craft glue to front of card, under flap.
4. Punch 1½" square from dark brown card stock.
5. Apply mug sticker and attach yarn with craft glue.
6. Stamp the word "chocolate" across the bottom of yellow card stock, using various sizes and styles of letters.
7. Stamp "hot" on other spots of yellow card stock.
8. Punch ½" holes in top center of card. Thread chocolate-colored ribbon and tie bow.

Building a Snowman

Materials

- Black fimo clay
- Craft glue
- Craft stick
- Cream card stock
- Embroidery flosses: red, green, and orange
- Excelsior
- Felt: red, green, and orange
- Large paint can
- Needle
- Page protector
- Patterned paper
- Pinking shears
- Red brad
- Red rickrack
- Round vellum tag
- Sewing machine
- Scissors
- Small zip-lock bag
- Snowflake charm
- Thread
- Wire

Can

1. For scarf, cut a 5" x 46" strip of green felt, two 5" x 5" squares of red felt, and two red primitive hearts.
2. Sew a red square to each end of the green strip, with the right sides together, and cut into fringe. Hand-stitch the two red hearts on the top side of scarf.
3. For mittens, double the red felt to cut two mittens, creating four mittens. (Refer to Mitten pattern on page 110.) Sew the wrong sides together, around the outside edge. Cut seam allowance down with pinking shears. Hand-stitch a star to the top of each mitten.
4. For ear muffs, double red felt and cut two circles, to create four circles. Sew the wrong sides together, around the outside edge, leaving small opening at top. Cut seam allowance down with pinking shears.
5. Cut a piece of wire about 11" long. Using a zigzag stitch, sew wire to small strip of green felt. Cut close to wire with pinking shears. Insert wire into small opening in each earmuff. Hand-stitch closed.
6. Cut two green primitive hearts and hand-stitch one to each muff.
7. For nose, double orange felt to cut two carrot shapes. Sew right sides together along long edge. Turn right side out.
8. Sew a running stitch with the orange floss along the top of carrot. Stuff with excelsior, glue the craft stick in place, and pull the threads tight.
9. For coal, sculpt "coal" shapes from clay and cook, following manufacturer's directions.
10. Place coal inside small zip-lock bag.
11. Place excelsior, mittens, scarf, nose, and bag of coal inside the can.
12. Attach the earmuffs to the top of the can with two pieces of wire on either side.

Label

1. Type or print text on solid card stock. Mount on patterned paper, then edge with rickrack. Laminate if desired.
2. Attach to front of can with craft glue.

Tag

1. Place snowflake charm on vellum tag.
2. Attach with red brad.

Box

1. Wrap box with maroon ribbon, attaching at top with craft glue.
2. Using glue gun, add feather to top and wrap with frosted floral berries.

Tag

1. Cut tag shape from white card stock.
2. Apply thin line of craft glue to edges of tag. Sprinkle with silver glitter. Let dry.
3. Glue snowflake charm to center of tag, on an angle. Glue feathers above and below it.
4. Punch hole in top and tie maroon ribbon through hole.

Card

1. Cut card from white card stock. Fold in half.
2. Add buckle to ribbon and attach to card with glue dots.
3. Apply thin line of craft glue to edges of card. Sprinkle with silver glitter. Let dry.
4. Add oval tag, Christmas bells, and "Happy Holidays" charms with craft glue. Let dry.

Materials

- ¼" hole punch
- Clear-drying craft glue
- Frosted floral berries
- Glue dots
- Glue gun
- Maroon wire-edged ribbon
- Metal charms: miniature belt buckle, oval tag, Christmas bell, snowflake, and "Happy holidays"
- Silver glitter
- White box
- White card stock
- White feather

Joy to the World

Materials

- ¼" hole punch
- 4½" round brown box
- Assorted flat-backed jewels
- Black embroidery floss
- Card stocks: yellow, red, white, and dark brown
- Craft glue
- Decorative brown paper
- Glue dots
- Gold mini brads
- Ink pads: black and gold
- Large alphabet stamps
- Maroon handmade paper
- Metallic gold string
- Miniature Christmas card
- Tulle
- White card stock

Box

1. Stamp Christmas saying around front of box. Let dry.
2. Glue strip of torn yellow card stock on angle to top of box lid. Stamp "Joy" on box lid.
3. Make poinsettia by tearing petals from maroon paper and securing with gold brads.
4. Attach poinsettia to box lid with glue dot. Glue gold string from end of card stock strip to just above center, using craft glue. Attach jewel to lid with glue dot.

Tag

1. Cut tag from white card stock.
2. Tear a small piece of red card stock and attach to top center of tag with glue stick.
3. Punch hole in top center of tag with ¼" hole punch.
4. Cover tag with thin coat of clear-drying glue.
5. Attach tulle to tag front. Let dry.
6. Dab gold ink pad over tag cover. Let dry.
7. Wrap gold string two times around bottom of tag.
8. Make a poinsettia, as described in box instructions.
9. Attach poinsettia, jewel, and small card with glue dots.
10. Tie gold string through hole.

Card

1. Cut card from dark brown card stock. Cover front with decorative brown paper, using glue stick.
2. Attach jewel to center-right edge with glue dot.
3. Wrap black thread around jewel and attach to back of card with glue dot. Cover glue with small paper circle.
4. Make poinsettia as described in box instructions above and attach to center of card with glue dot.

Materials

- 2 styles of coordinating decorative green polka-dotted paper
- Card stocks: dark green, red, and speckled cream
- Christmas light stickers
- Dark green box
- Glue stick
- Gold mesh ribbon
- Gold wire ribbon
- Merry Christmas plastic stone
- Permanent marker

Box

1. About 1" from top of front of box, curl wire ribbon in various spots, stopping occasionally to attach stickers, making it appear as if it is the wire to a string of lights.
2. Add large, gold mesh ribbon bow to top of box.

Tag

1. Cut piece of gold wire ribbon about 6" long.
2. Place about ¼" length of each end of string under top of bulb sticker.
3. Layer another sticker on top, sticky sides together.
4. Write recipient's name on tag, using permanent marker.

Card

1. Cut two cards from polka-dotted paper.
2. Glue wrong sides together. Fold in half.
3. Attach dark green card stock to lower half of card front.
4. Add Christmas light stickers and wire in same manner as described in box instructions above.
5. Attach "Merry Christmas" plastic stone with glue dots on lower-right corner of card.
6. For inside of card, cut cream card stock 1" smaller on all sides than card.
7. Mount on dark green card stock, leaving border of about ¹⁄₁₆" all around.
8. Add two different-colored Christmas lights stickers to upper-left corner of cream card stock.
9. Glue to inside of card.

merry christmas

Christmas Tree

Container

1. Place the ornaments in the small jar.
2. Attach the tree to the top of the jar with industrial strength glue.
3. Wrap the garland around the base of the tree and the top of the jar.
4. Print holiday greetings onto vellum strip and attach to ribbon with gold brads.

Tag

1. Using the alphabet beads and wire, create greeting and attach to wire reindeer.
2. Attach to the tree.

Materials

- 18" Christmas tree
- Alphabet beads
- Gold brads
- Gold wire
- Industrial-strength glue
- Ribbon
- Small glass jar with flat lid
- Small glass ornaments
- Vellum
- Wire Christmas garland
- Wire-edged holiday ribbon
- Wire reindeer

Xmas Cookie Basket

Materials

- 6 small cookie cutters
- Buttons
- Card stocks: white and brown
- Cheesecloth
- Cotton Christmas ribbon
- Excelsior
- Gingerbread cookie mix
- Gingerbread man cutout
- Glue gun
- Large batter bowl
- Pop dot
- Raffia
- Red patterned paper
- Rolling pin
- Sewing machine
- White frosting

Container

1. String cookie cutters through ribbon and wrap around bowl. Add a small dollop of glue to ribbon after every cutter to secure.
2. Tie off ribbon and attach button over knot.
3. Remove cookie mix from the box. Type cooking instructions from the box onto white card stock. Mount on patterned paper and brown card stock. Sew to front of cheesecloth.
4. Sew the two sides of the cheesecloth to make a bag. Tie two pieces of raffia, one at the top and one at the bottom. Glue on button.
5. Using the pop dot, attach the gingerbread man. Glue button to the front.
6. Make a label for the frosting in the same manner.
7. Stuff bowl with excelsior and add ingredients.

Tag

1. Print message on white card stock and mount on patterned paper and brown card stock.
2. Sew around edges.
3. Glue bottom to front of tag.
4. Hang tag from rolling pin with raffia and clothespin.

Gingerbread
Cookie mix

Add 1/4 cup water, 2 tbls flour,
2 tbls, melted butter. Mix well
in bowl. Roll out onto a floured
surface. Cut out in the desired
shapes. Cook in a 375-degree o
for 8-10 minutes. Let cool.
njoy!

Frosting

Merry Christmas
Angie
Love, Darci

Materials

- 12" x 12" square of gold-embossed card stock
- Glue gun
- Miniature gold frame
- Miscellaneous trims (tassel, flowers, etc.)
- Scrap of cream card stock

Bag

1. On the reverse side of the gold card stock, draw a half circle from one end to opposite end, getting as close as you can to the end of the paper to create a cone shape. Cut along the line of the circle.
2. Using a glue gun, carefully glue the ends together, slightly overlapping so the glue doesn't show.
3. Decorate the cone with trim, flowers, and tassel.

Tag

1. Print message on cream card stock.
2. Cut to fit inside gold frame.
3. Glue to front of card.

Credits

Border Paper Designers:

7gypsies: 28, 44, 76, 82, 112

All About Paper Co.: 120

All My Memories: 118

Amscan: 106

Anna Griffin: 26, 36

Autumn Leaves: 40

Colors by Design: 72

Creative Imaginations: 112

Cynthea Sandoval for Doodlebug Design, Inc.: 46, 60

Deborah Rodgers for Design Originals: 20

Déjà Views: 50

Deni Mechelle for Daisy D's: 9, 14

EK Success Ltd.: 122

Frances Meyer, Inc.: 22, 24, 48, 90

K&Company, LLC: 58, 80, 92, 101, 114

Karen Foster Design: 38, 42, 124

Karla Eisenach for Sweetwater: 86

Kathy Distefano Griffiths for Provo Craft: 34

Kopp Design: 5

Mary Engelbreit: 17

NRN Designs: 64

Paper Loft: 100

Printworks: 96

Provo Craft: 70

Robyn Pandolph for Daisy D's: 109

Sarah Lugg for The Paper Company: 88

The Paper Company: 126

Contact information for these designers may be found on Chapelle's web site at: www.chapelleltd.com.

Metric Equivalency Charts

inches to millimeters and centimeters													yards to meters									
inches	mm	cm	inches	cm	inches	cm	yards	meters	yards	meters	yards	meters	yards	meters	yards	meters
⅛	3	0.3	9	22.9	30	76.2	⅛	0.11	2⅛	1.94	4⅛	3.77	6⅛	5.60	8⅛	7.43
¼	6	0.6	10	25.4	31	78.7	⅛	0.11	2⅛	1.94	4⅛	3.77	6⅛	5.60	8⅛	7.43
½	13	1.3	12	30.5	33	83.8	¼	0.23	2¼	2.06	4¼	3.89	6¼	5.72	8¼	7.54
⅝	16	1.6	13	33.0	34	86.4	⅜	0.34	2⅜	2.17	4⅜	4.00	6⅜	5.83	8⅜	7.66
¾	19	1.9	14	35.6	35	88.9	½	0.46	2½	2.29	4½	4.11	6½	5.94	8½	7.77
⅞	22	2.2	15	38.1	36	91.4	⅝	0.57	2⅝	2.40	4⅝	4.23	6⅝	6.06	8⅝	7.89
1	25	2.5	16	40.6	37	94.0	¾	0.69	2¾	2.51	4¾	4.34	6¾	6.17	8¾	8.00
1¼	32	3.2	17	43.2	38	96.5	⅞	0.80	2⅞	2.63	4⅞	4.46	6⅞	6.29	8⅞	8.12
1½	38	3.8	18	45.7	39	99.1	1	0.91	3	2.74	5	4.57	7	6.40	9	8.23
1¾	44	4.4	19	48.3	40	101.6	1⅛	1.03	3⅛	2.86	5⅛	4.69	7⅛	6.52	9⅛	8.34
2	51	5.1	20	50.8	41	104.1	1¼	1.14	3¼	2.97	5¼	4.80	7¼	6.63	9¼	8.46
2½	64	6.4	21	53.3	42	106.7	1⅜	1.26	3⅜	3.09	5⅜	4.91	7⅜	6.74	9⅜	8.57
3	76	7.6	22	55.9	43	109.2	1½	1.37	3½	3.20	5½	5.03	7½	6.86	9½	8.69
3½	89	8.9	23	58.4	44	111.8	1⅝	1.49	3⅝	3.31	5⅝	5.14	7⅝	6.97	9⅝	8.80
4	102	10.2	24	61.0	45	114.3	1¾	1.60	3¾	3.43	5¾	5.26	7¾	7.09	9¾	8.92
4½	114	11.4	25	63.5	46	116.8	1⅞	1.71	3⅞	3.54	5⅞	5.37	7⅞	7.20	9⅞	9.03
5	127	12.7	26	66.0	47	119.4	2	1.83	4	3.66	6	5.49	8	7.32	10	9.14
6	152	15.2	27	68.6	48	121.9										
7	178	17.8	28	71.1	49	124.5										
8	203	20.3	29	73.7	50	127.0										

Index